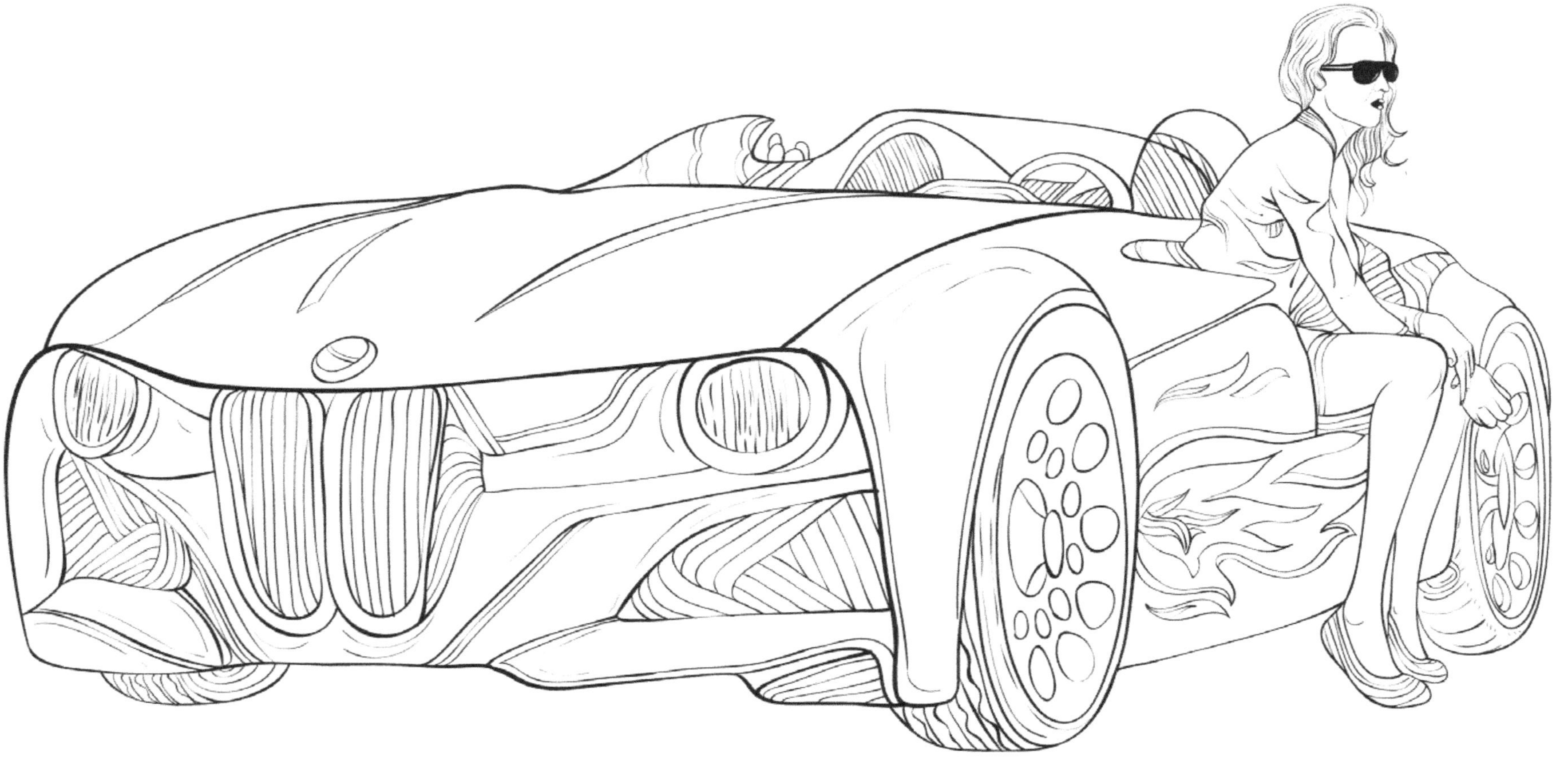

Where are your Pees and Queans honey-ass? How cum you swear like pooing behind the wheel? Oh dear, I'm so fucking confused.

Illustrated by:
    Mandala & Caricature Illustration
    Joshua Lazana Lagman and Jade Villaremo

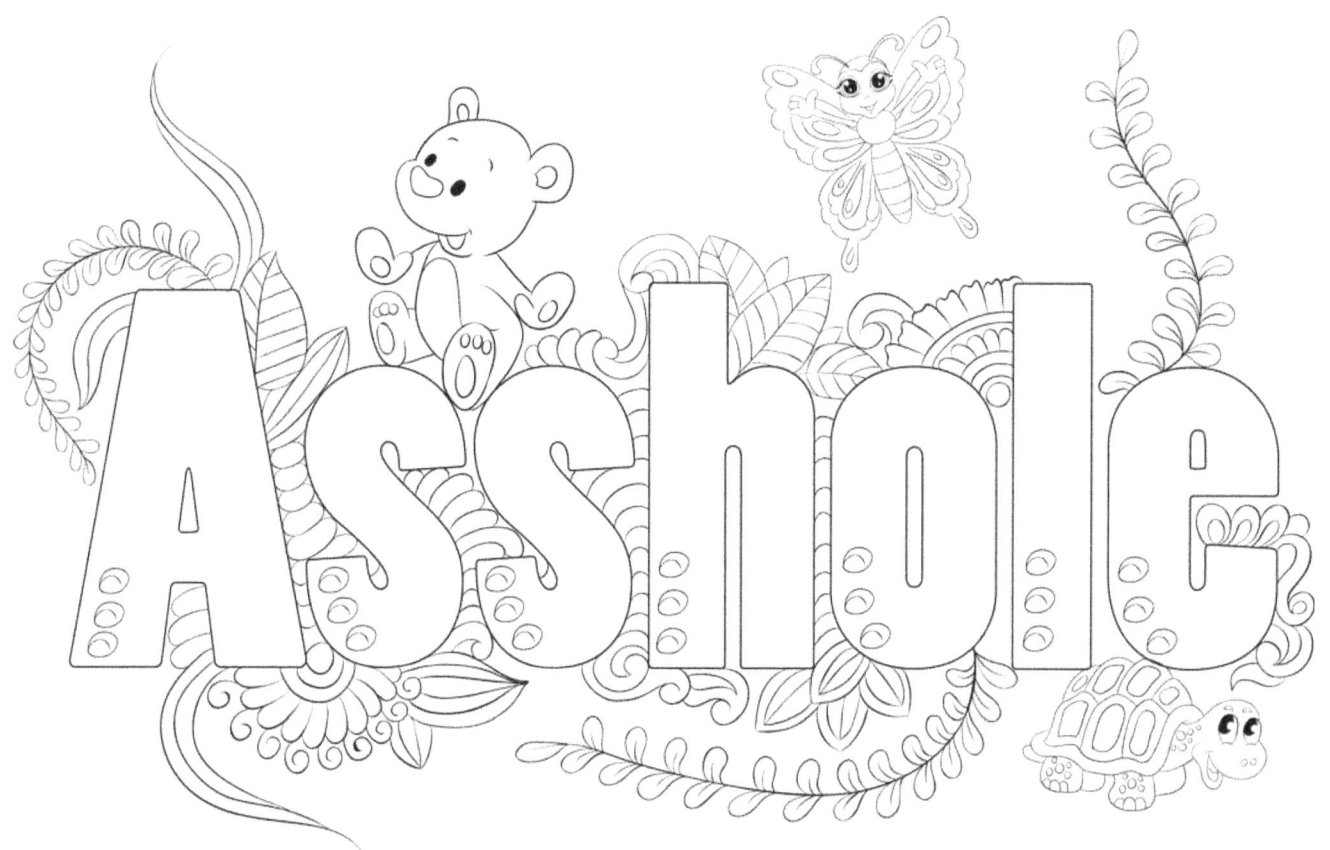

I fuck'n wish I could cut down on my swearing but I cunt.
So... fuck you!

Please stop swearing, dear. Or I'll have to wash your fucking mouth.

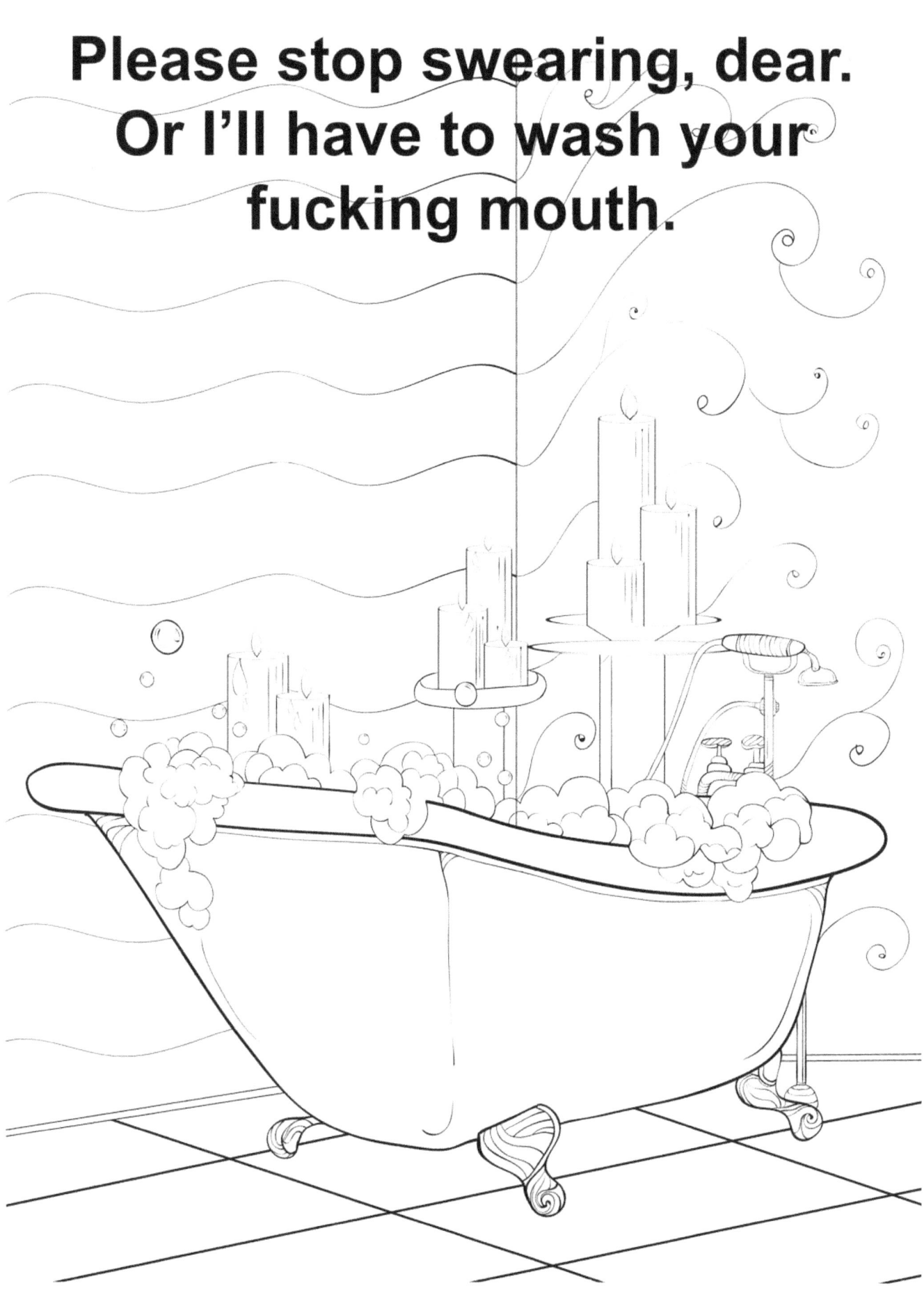

Yeah, yeah, tell me you love your day job. You love the paychecks, asshole!

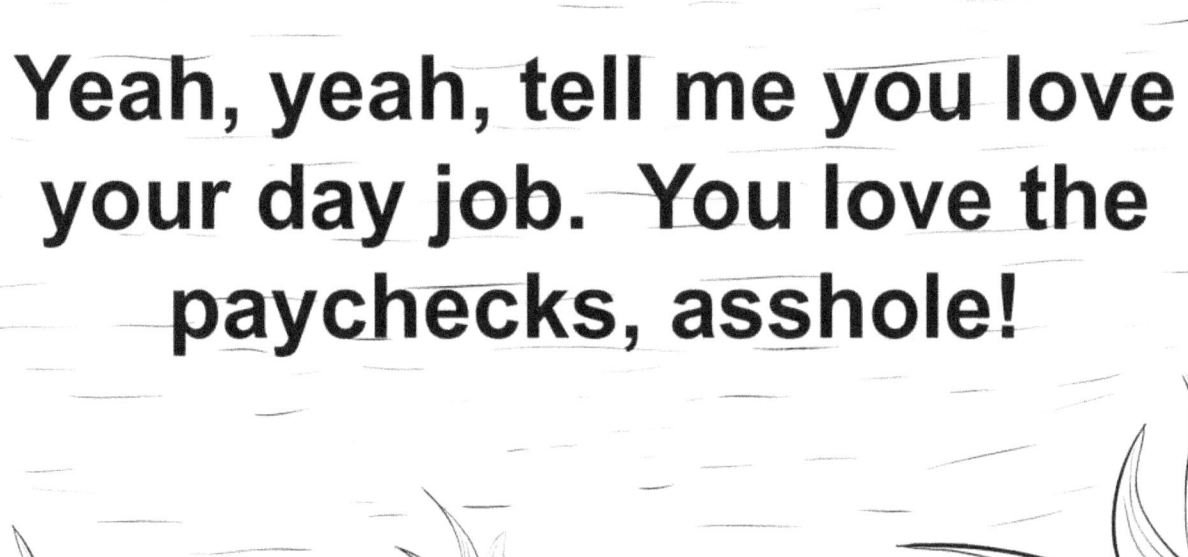

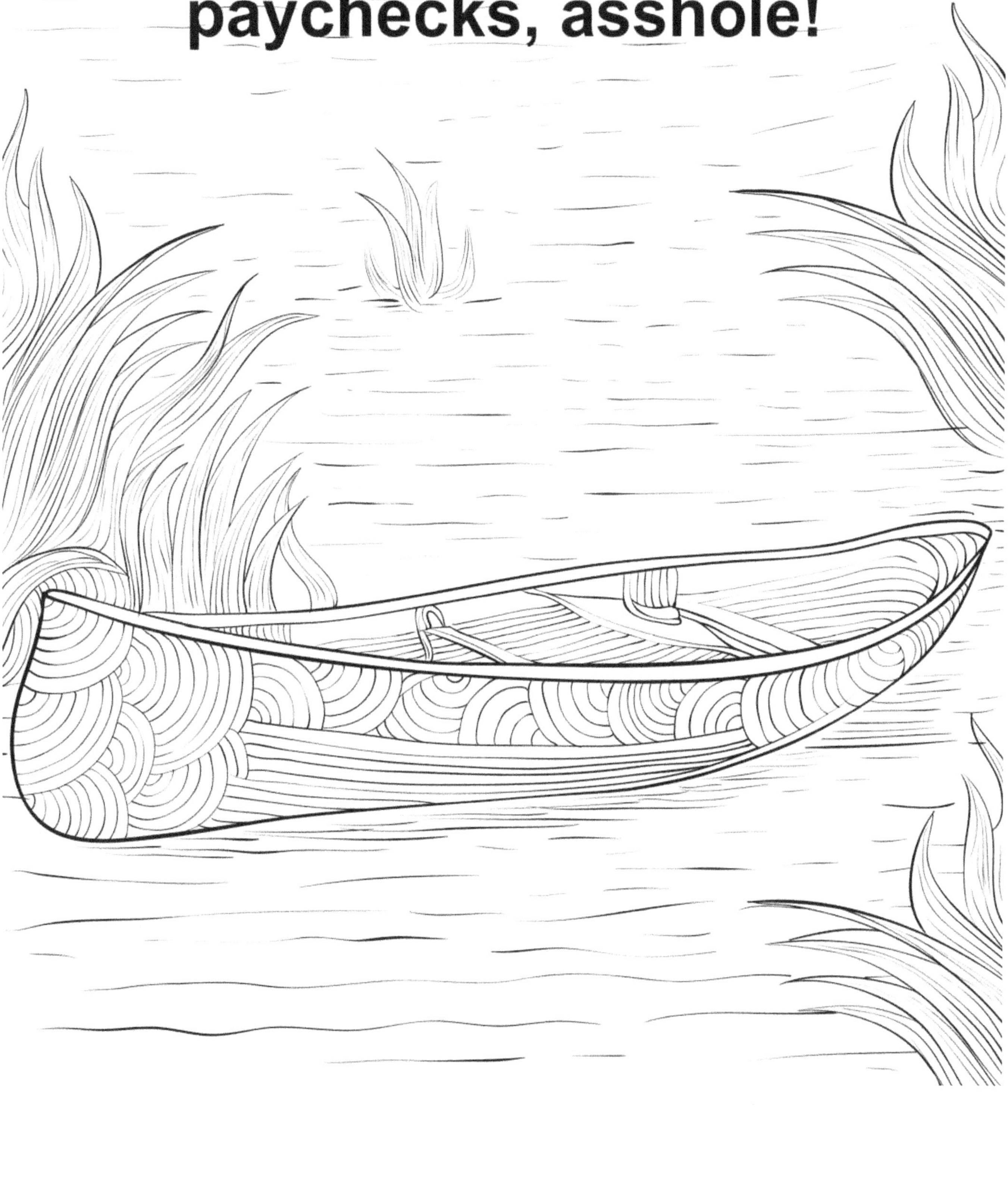

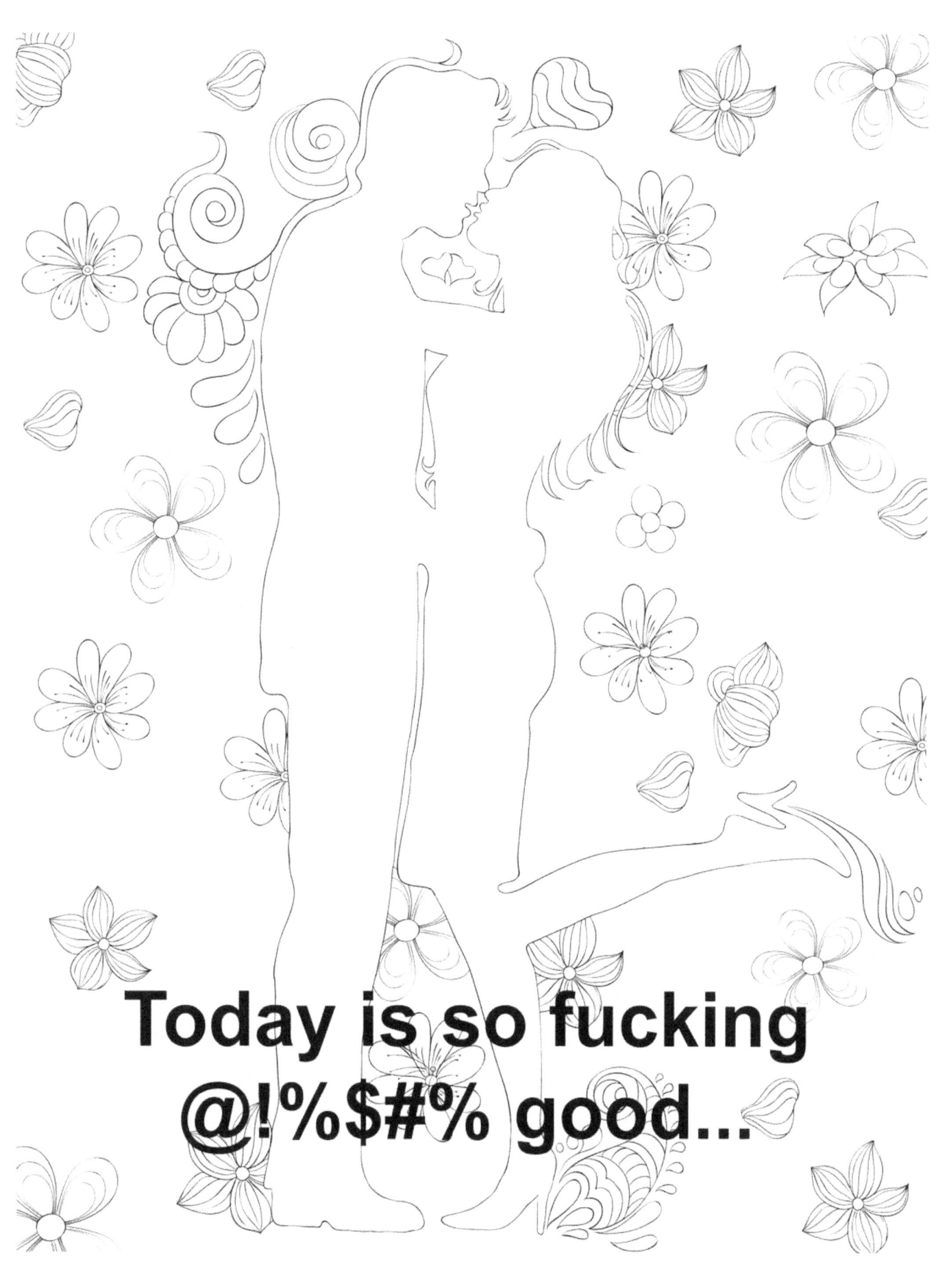

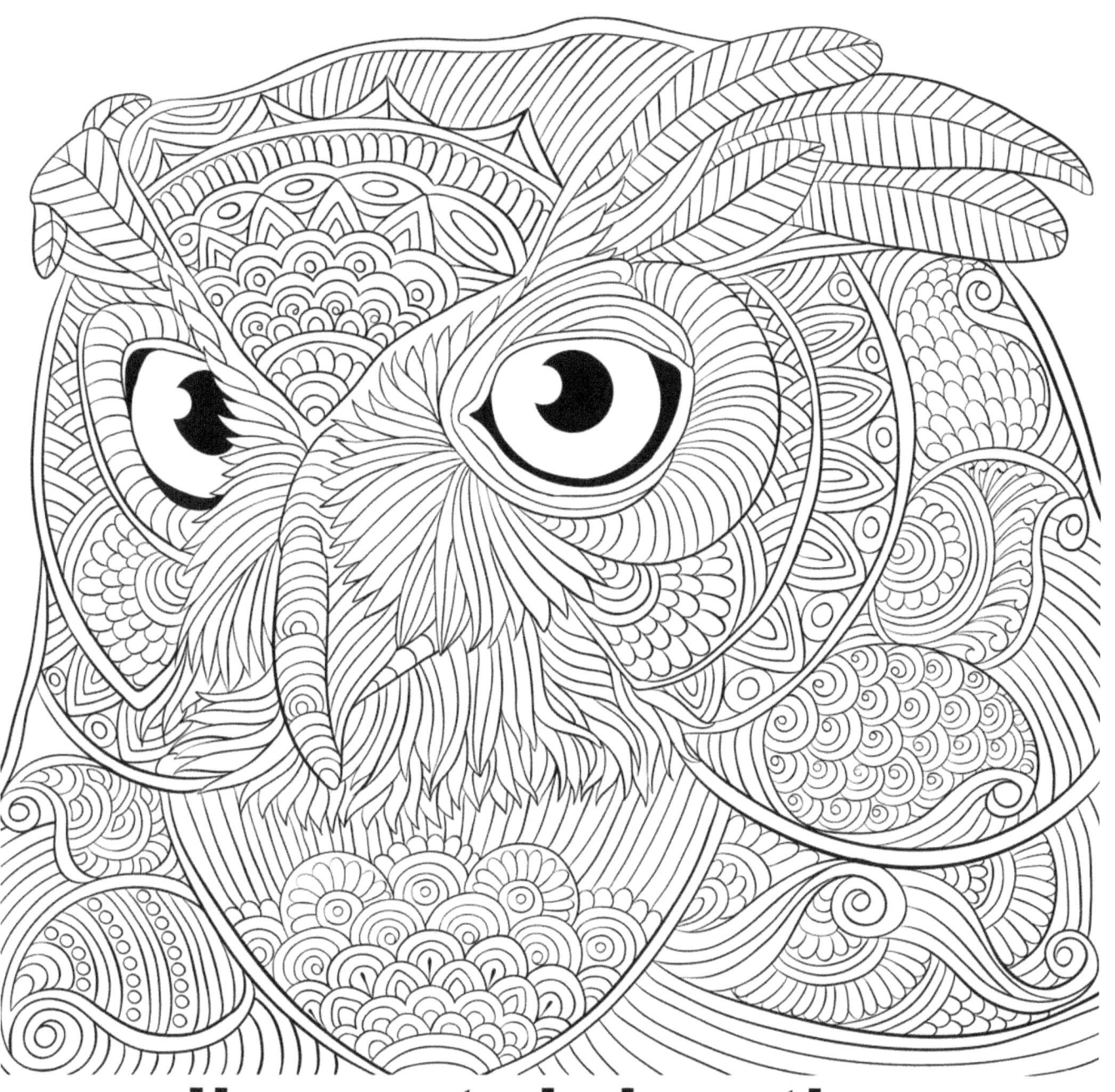

I'm not doing the shit today. So go fuck off.

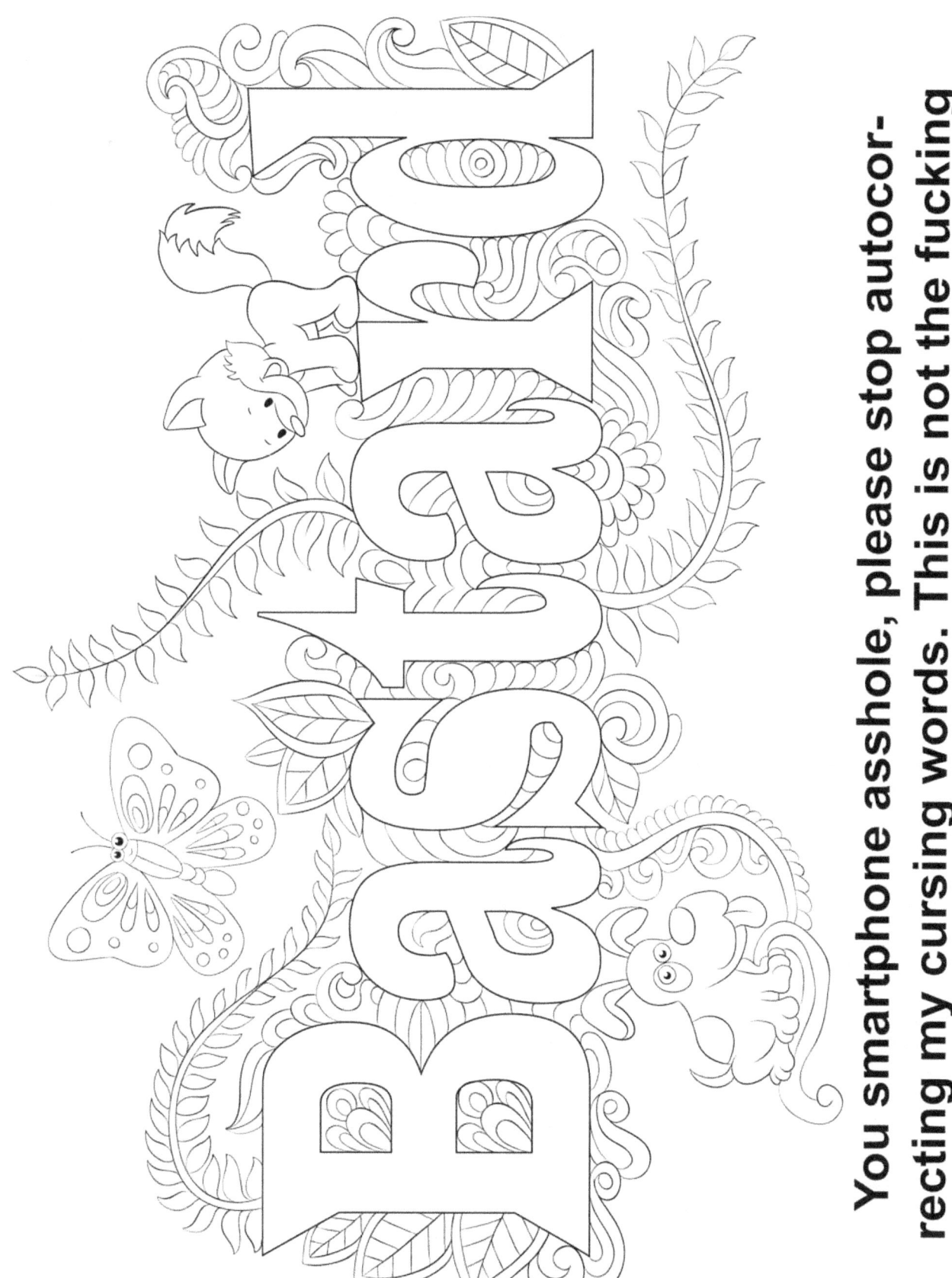

You smartphone asshole, please stop autocorrecting my cursing words. This is not the fucking feature I paid big bucks for.

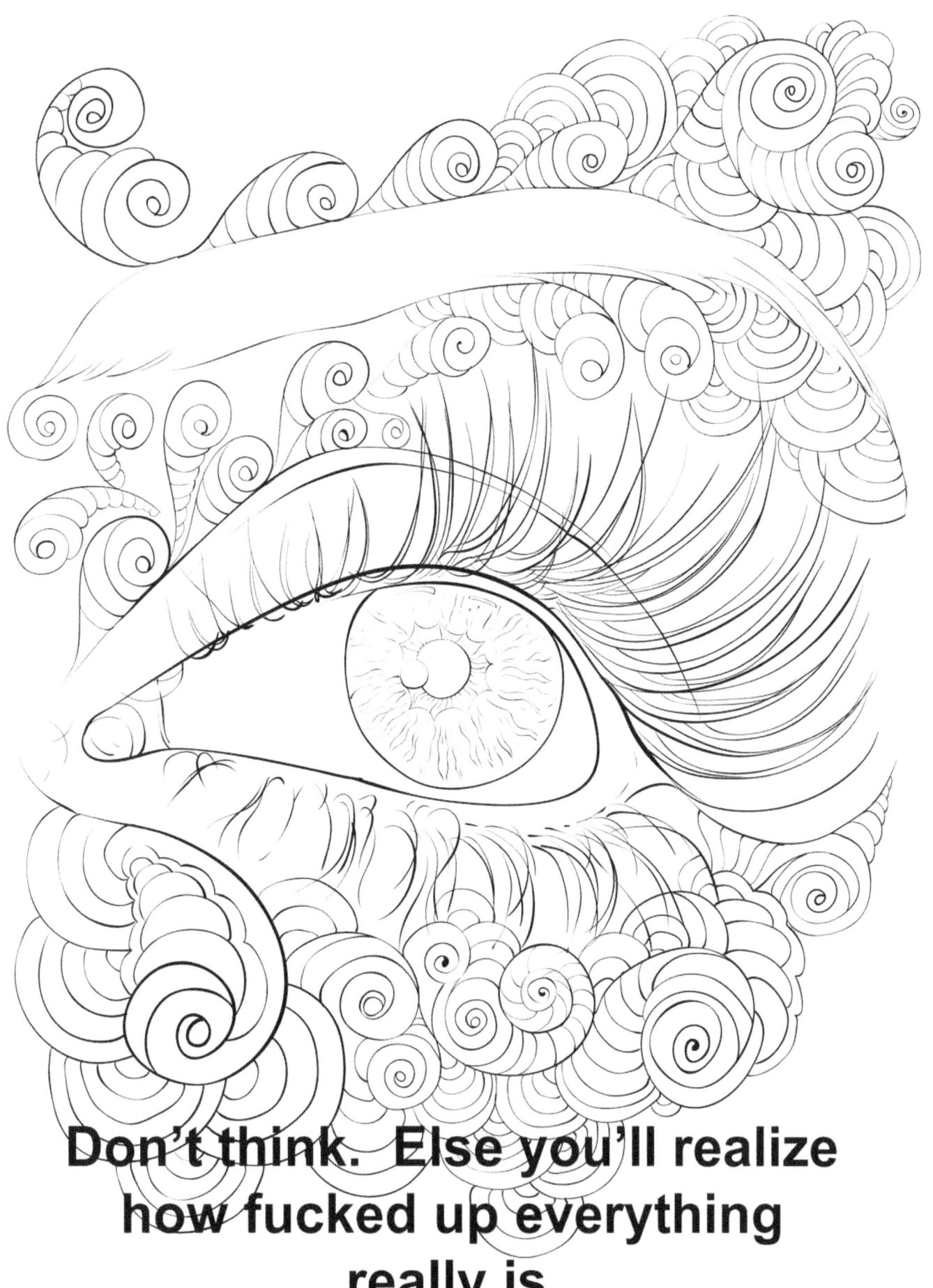

Don't think. Else you'll realize
how fucked up everything
really is.

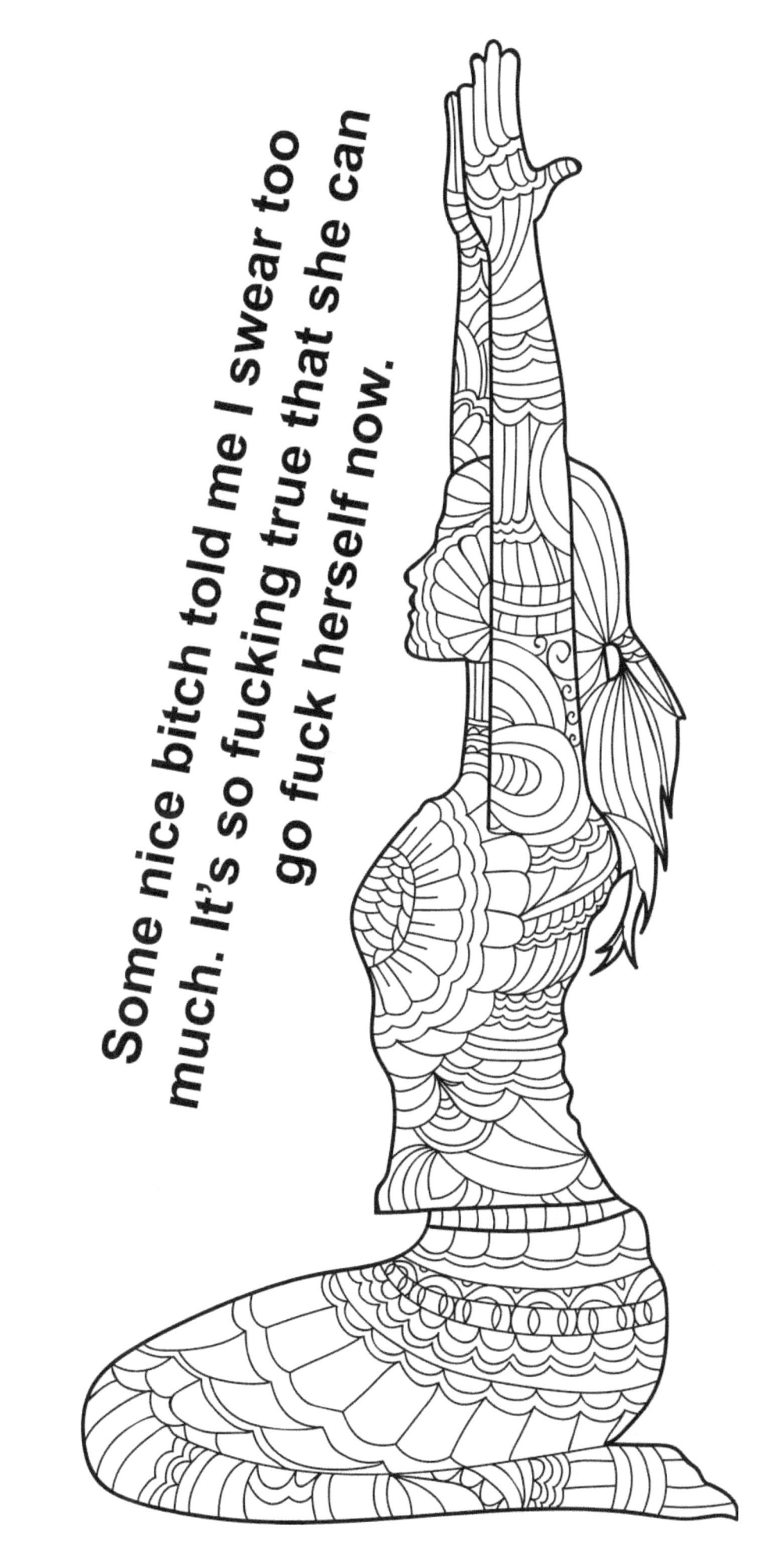

Some nice bitch told me I swear too much. It's so fucking true that she can go fuck herself now.

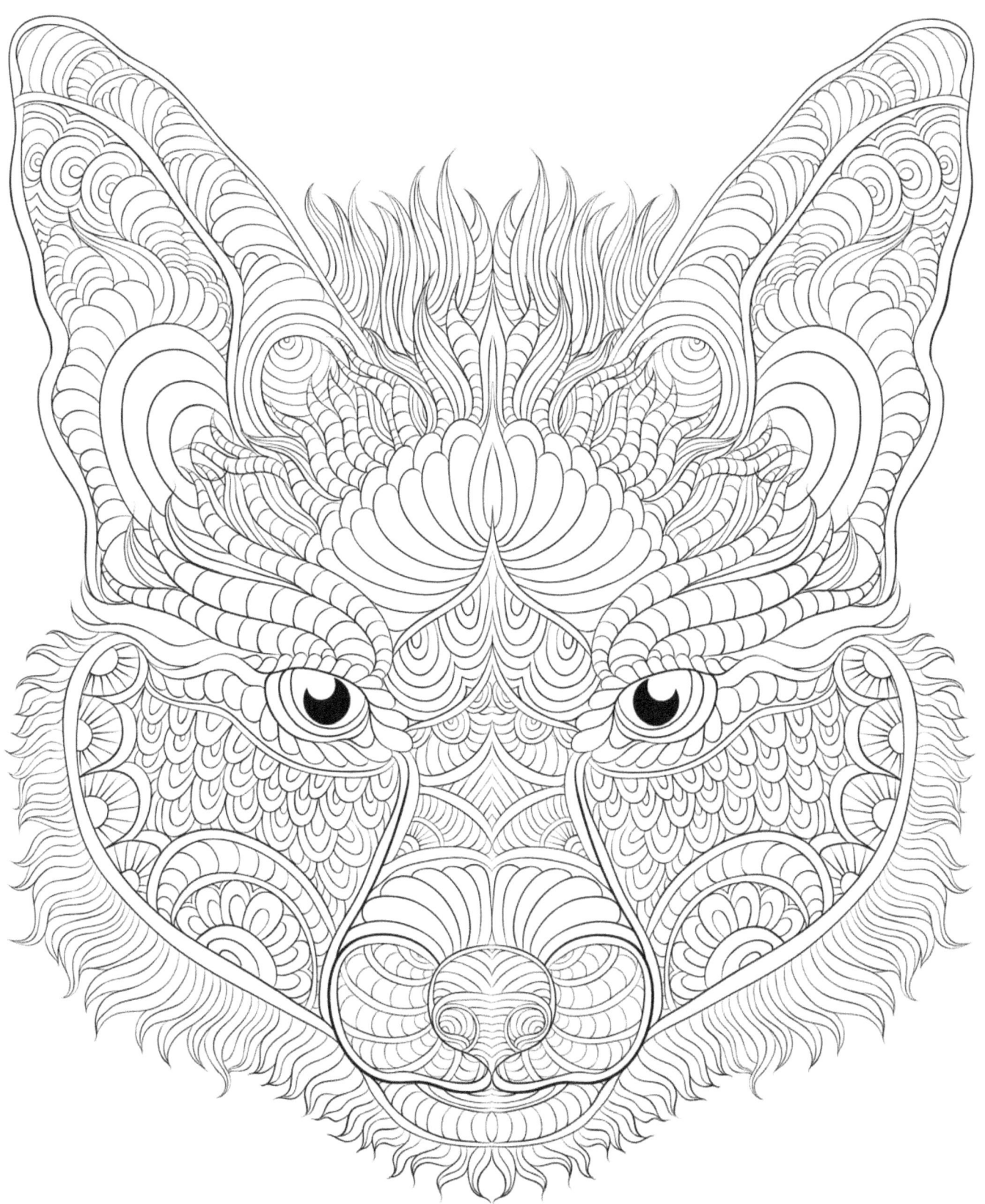

**The good news is that you won't die.
The bad news is that we don't know
what the fuck is wrong with you.**

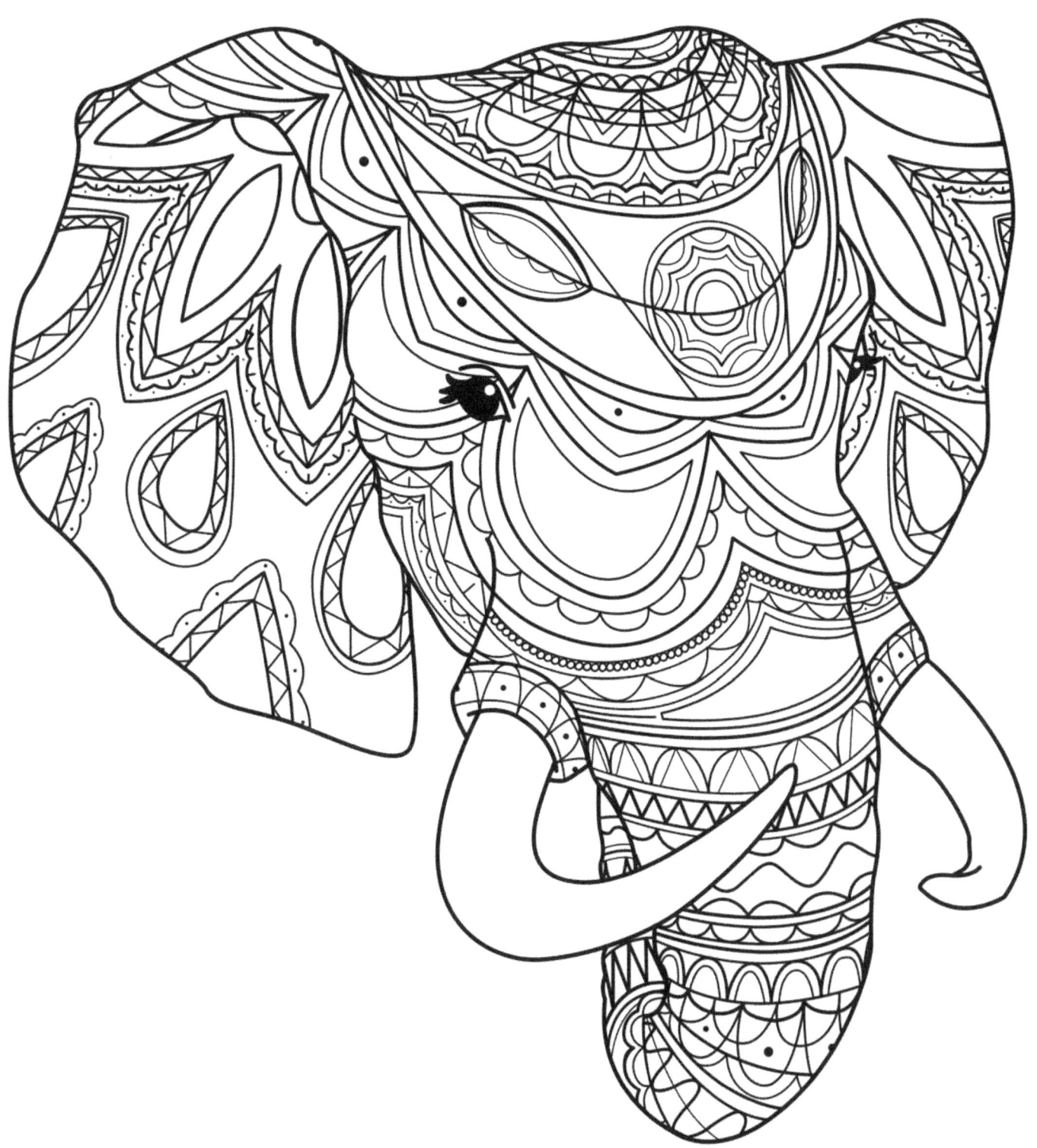

I hate when people tell me that swearing is not necessary. It's like fucking telling me that breathing is not necessary.

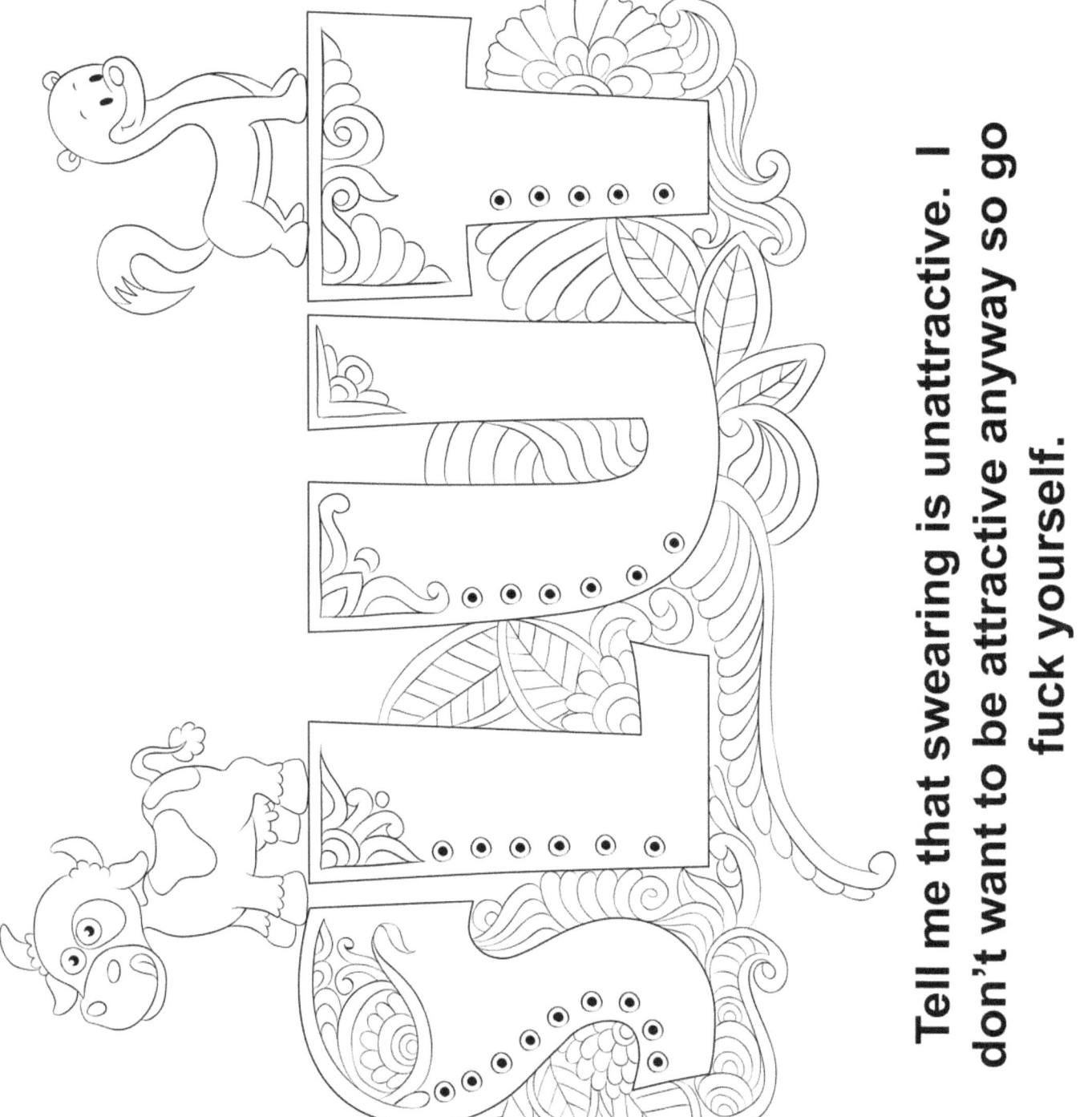

Tell me that swearing is unattractive. I don't want to be attractive anyway so go fuck yourself.

You think "go away" is rude, huh?

Fine. Go fuck off then.

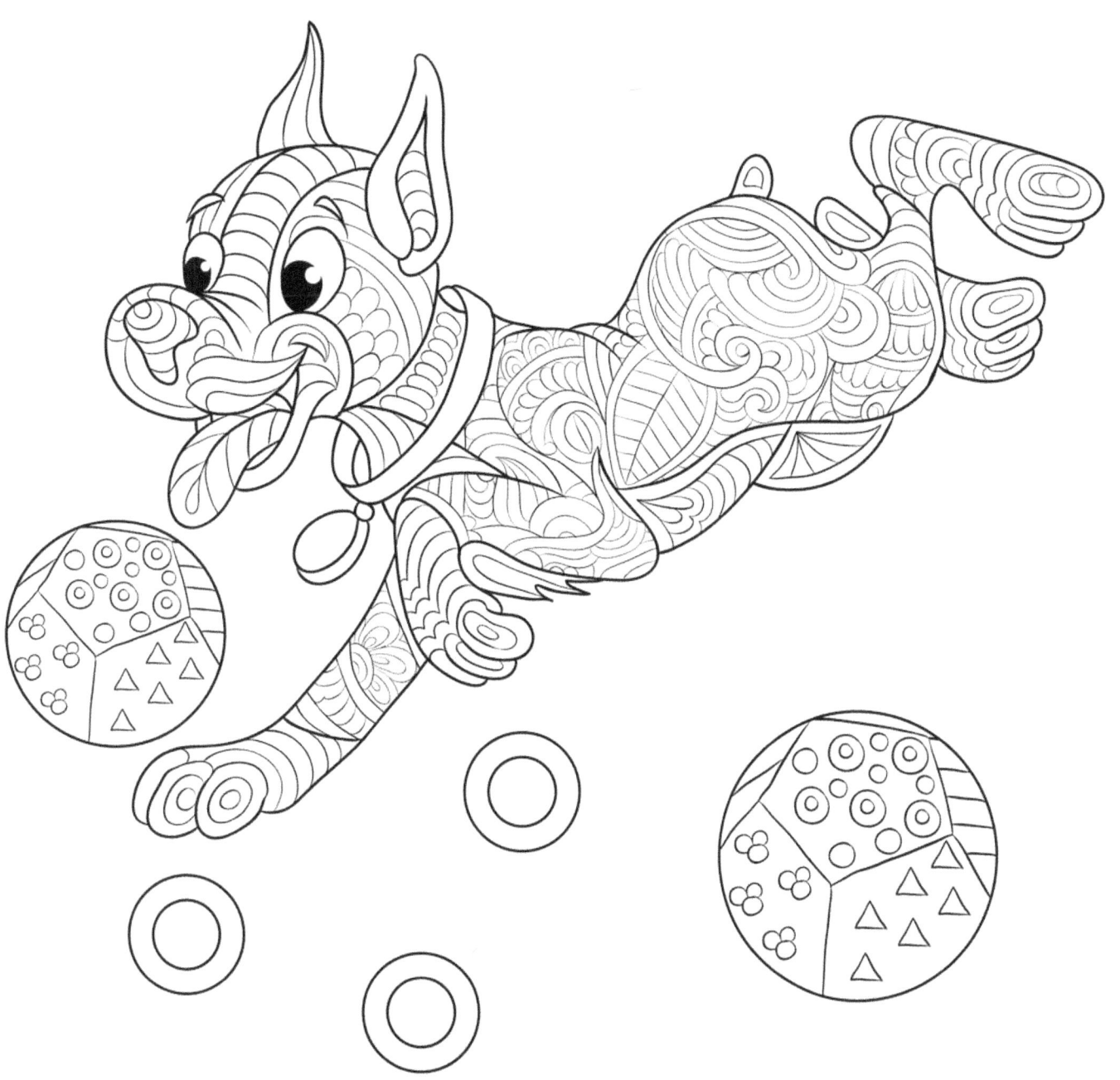

The reason I swear so much is because
you're too fucking adorable.

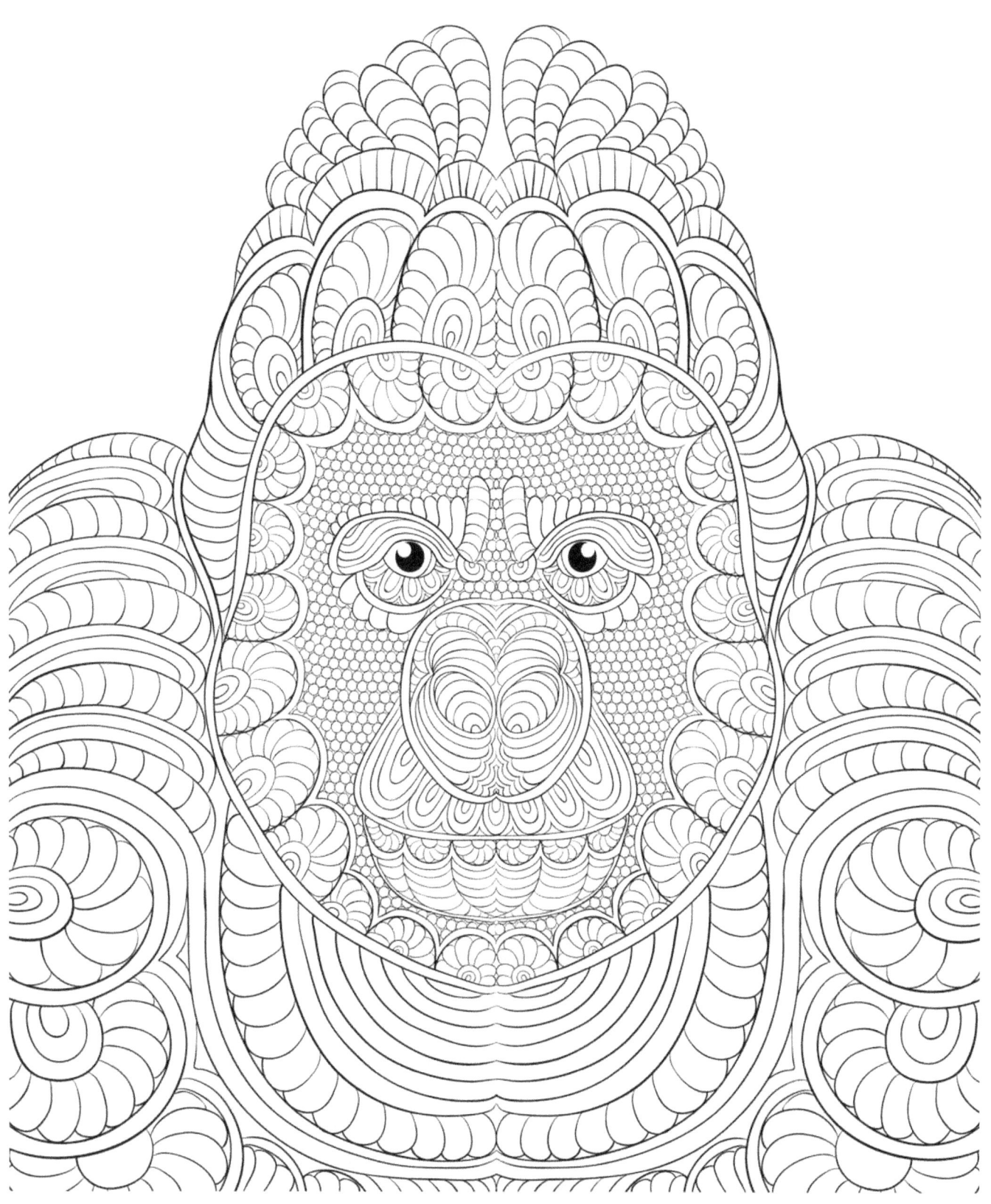

**Say whatever you want honey-cum.
I'm just sitting here masturbating.**

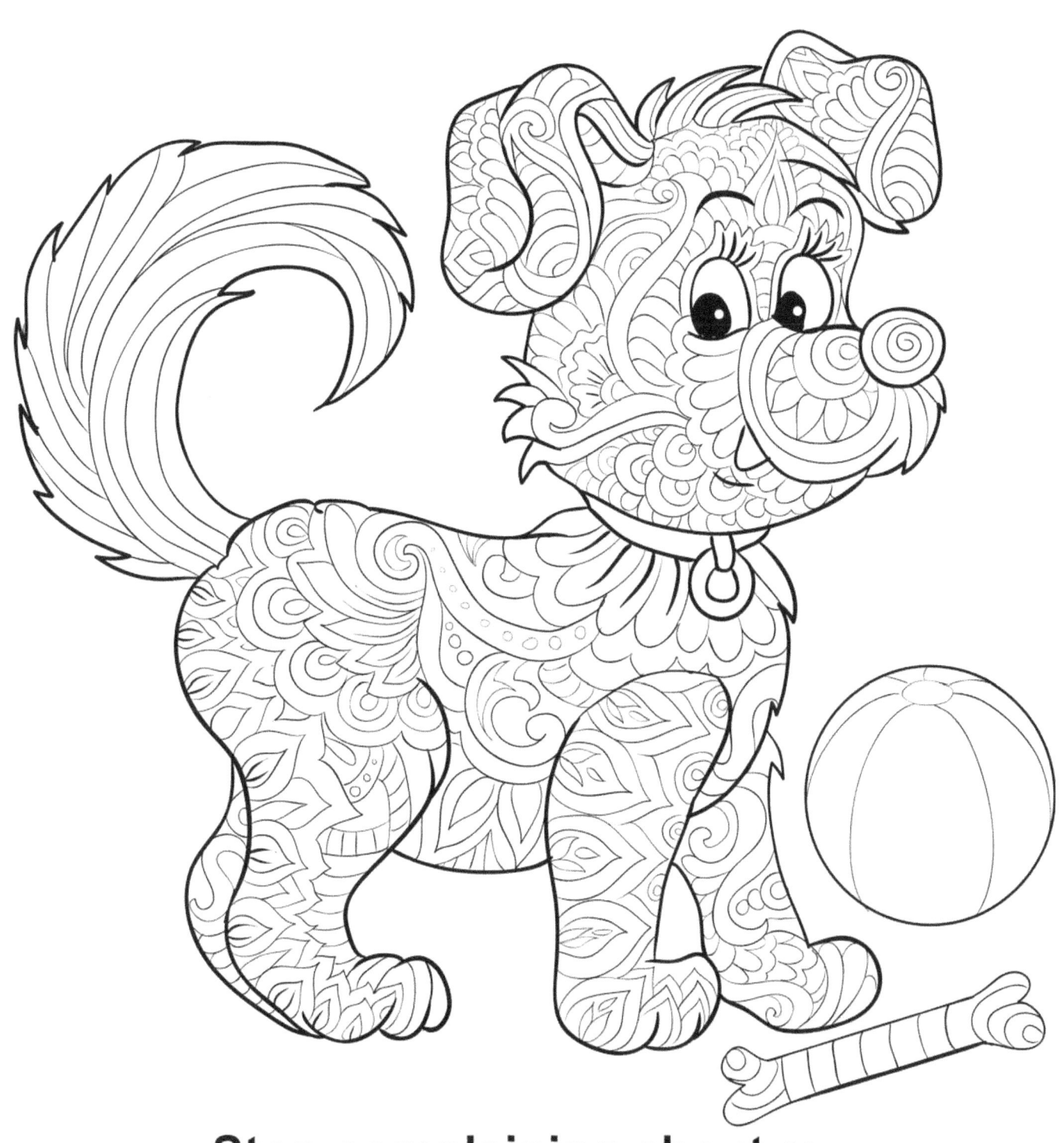

Stop complaining about my swearing. I got your fucking attention, didn't I?

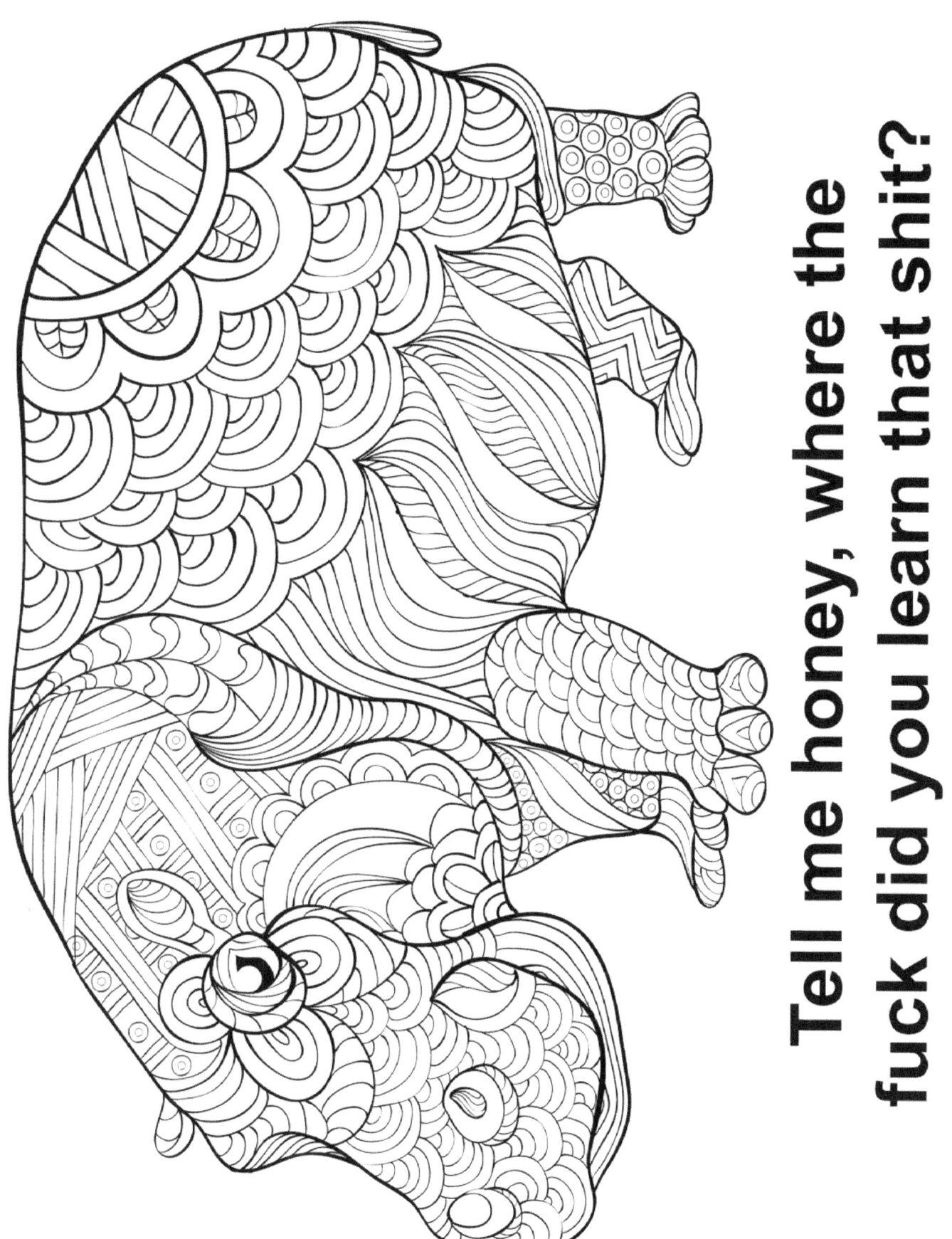

Tell me honey, where the
fuck did you learn that shit?

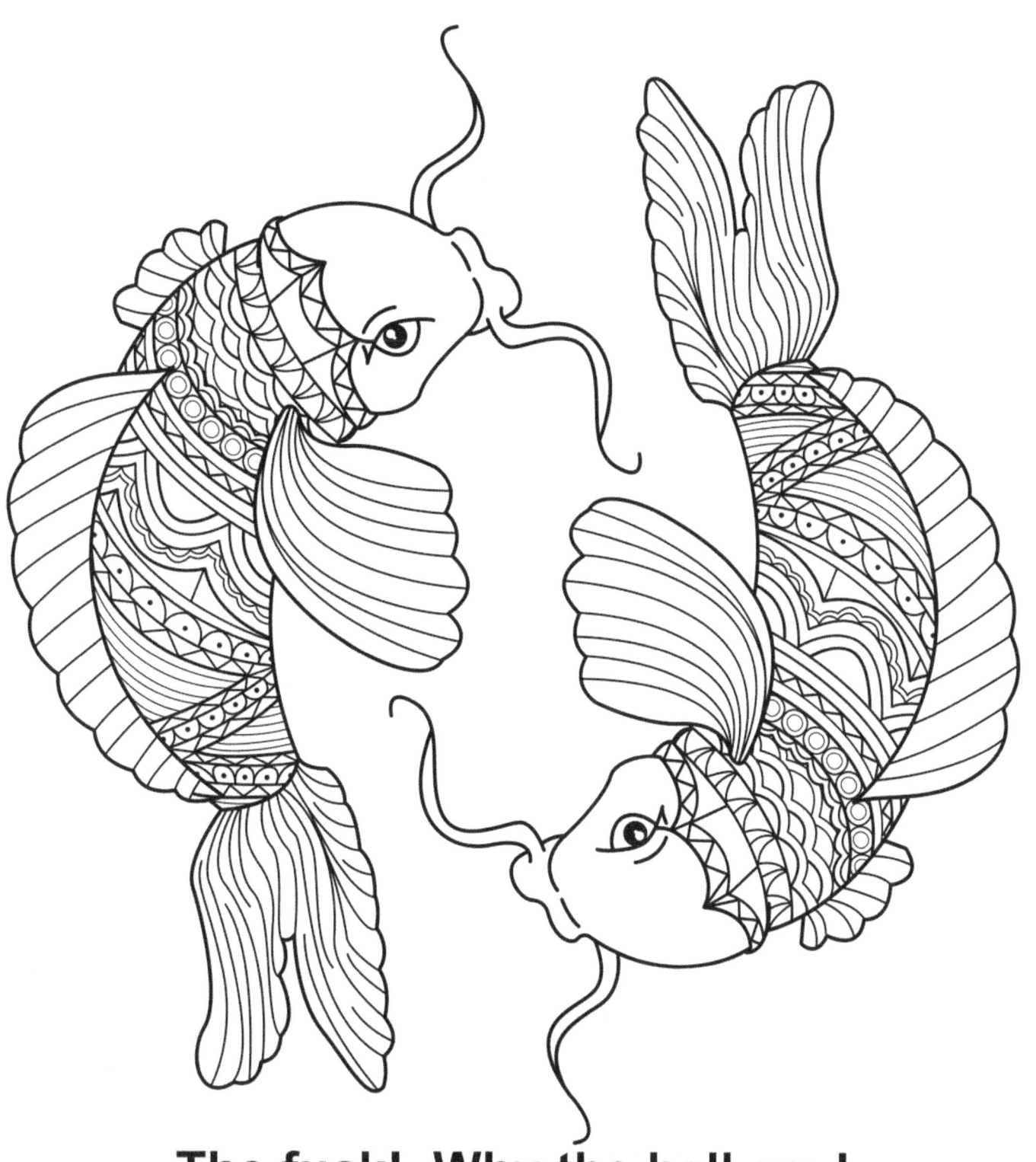

The fuck! Why the hell am I still single?

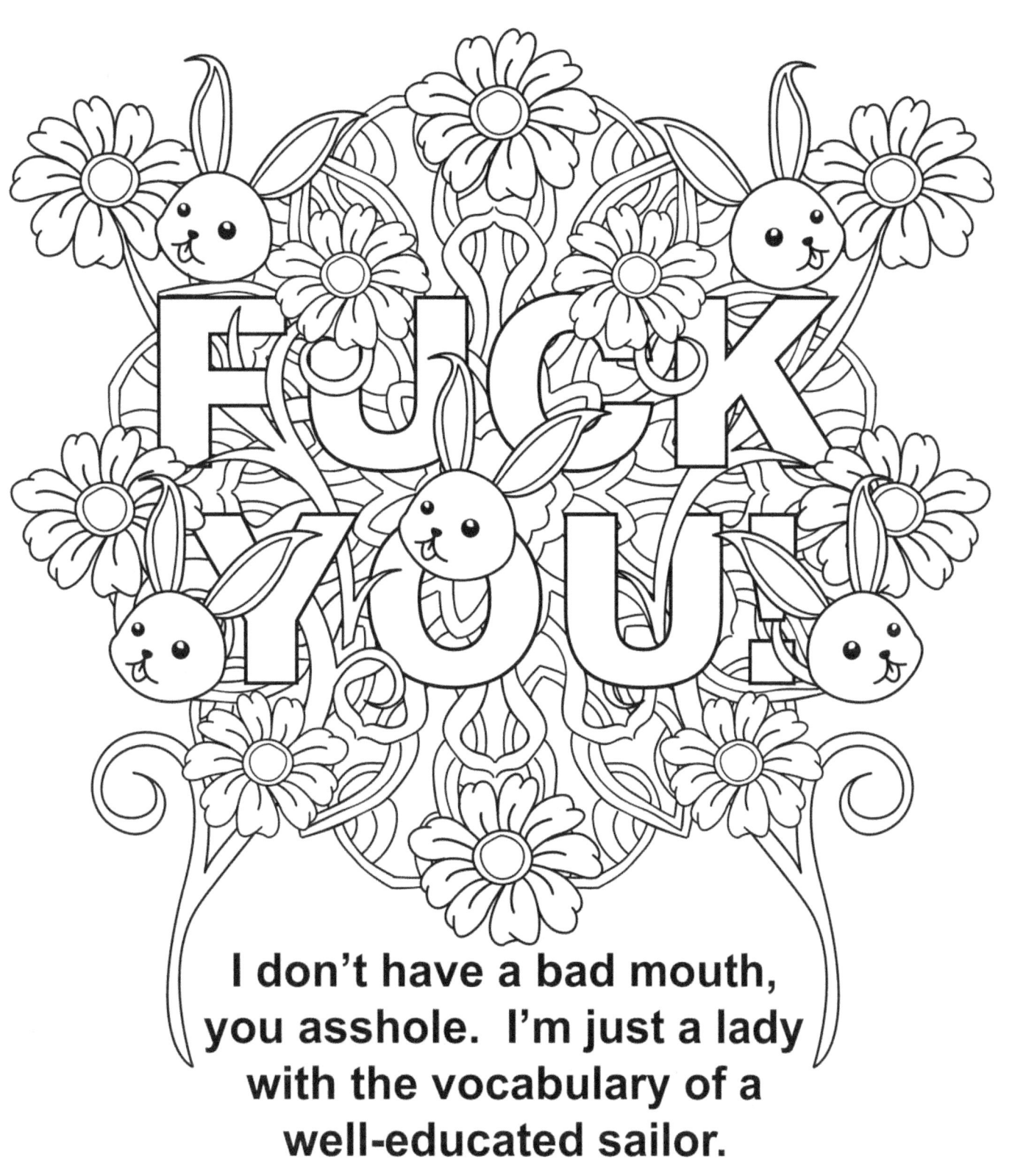

I don't have a bad mouth,
you asshole. I'm just a lady
with the vocabulary of a
well-educated sailor.

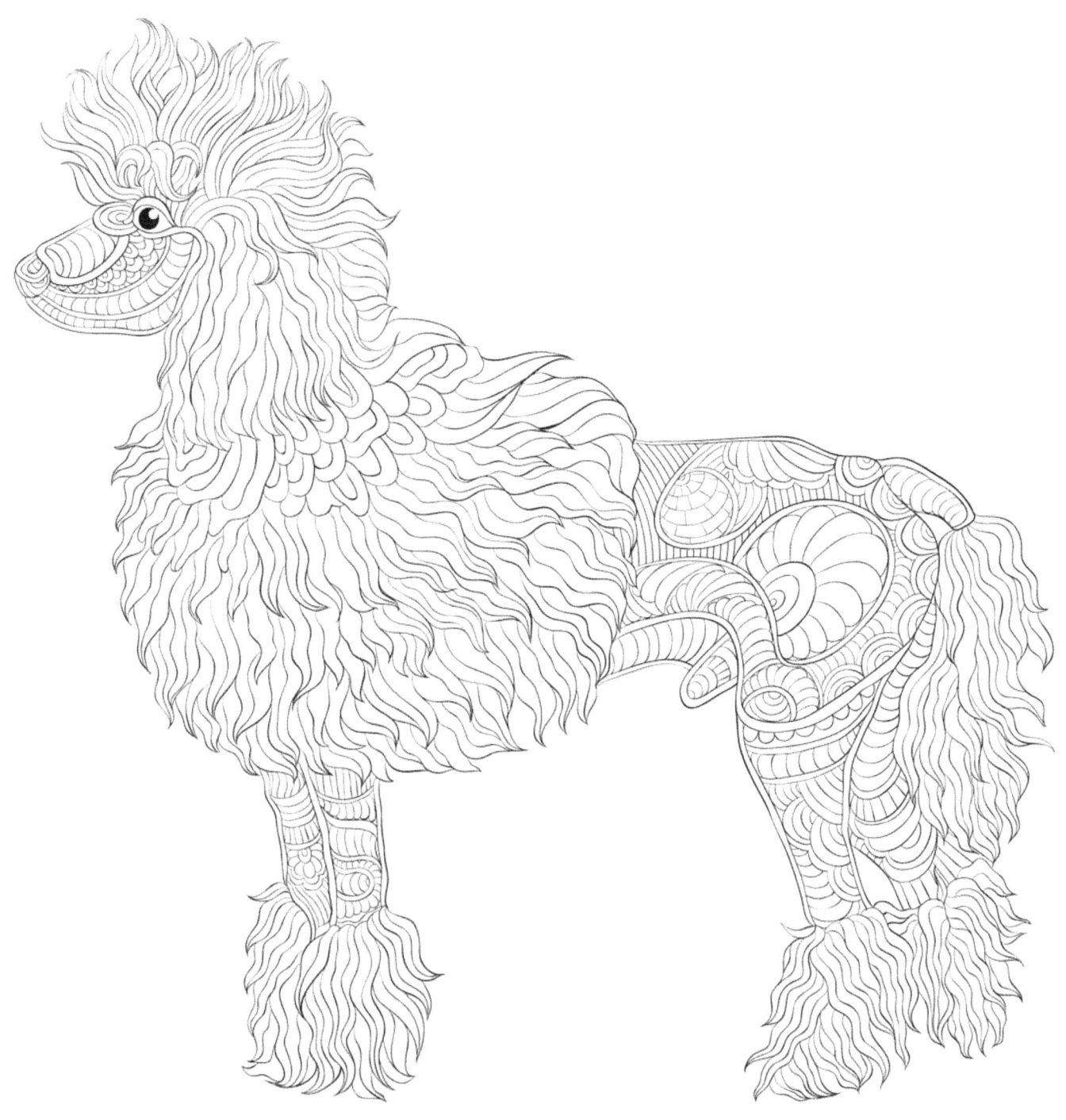

He's so fucking bad that he
lies even when he swears.

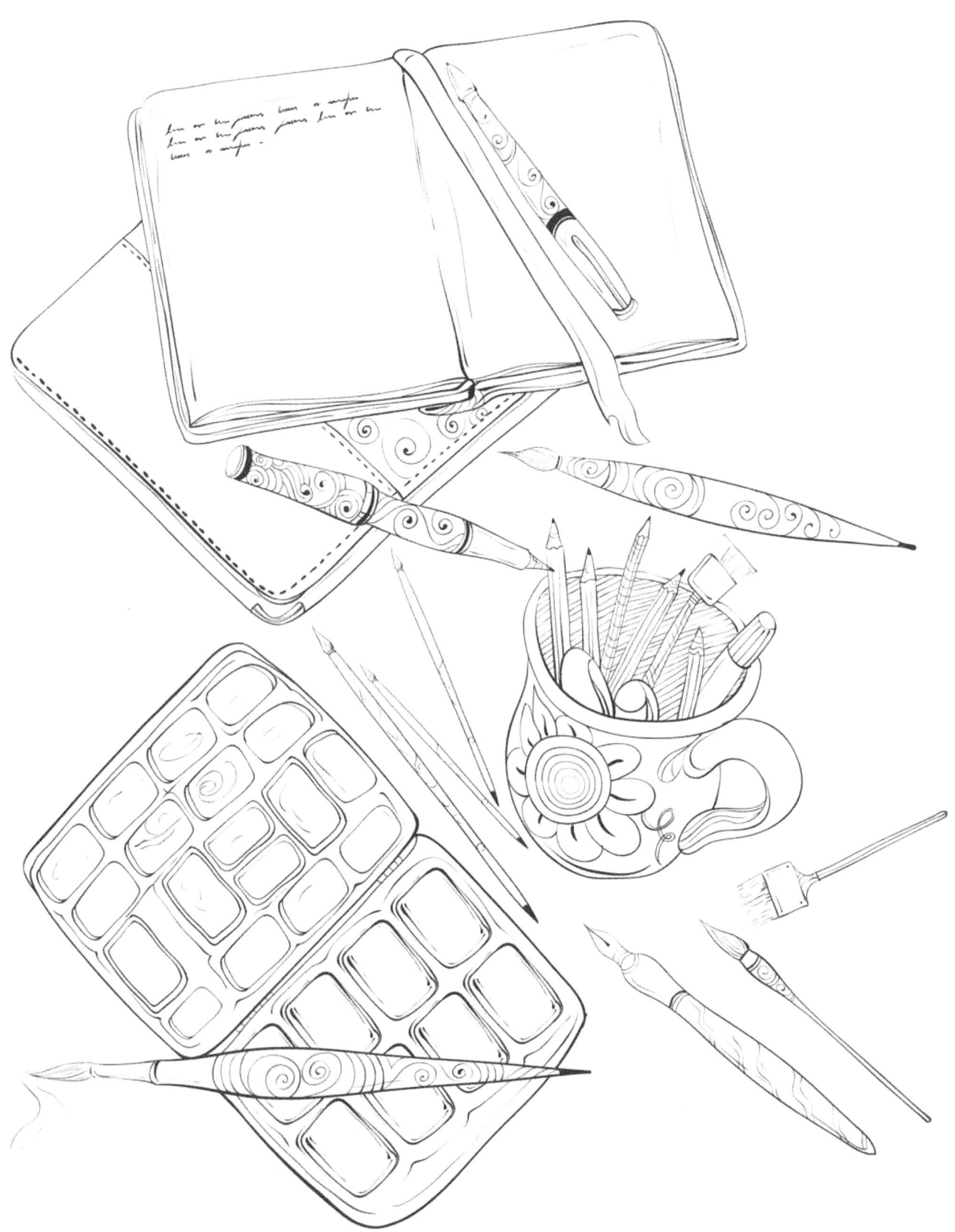

I can stop swearing if I can
find my goddamn shit bitch
mouthwash.

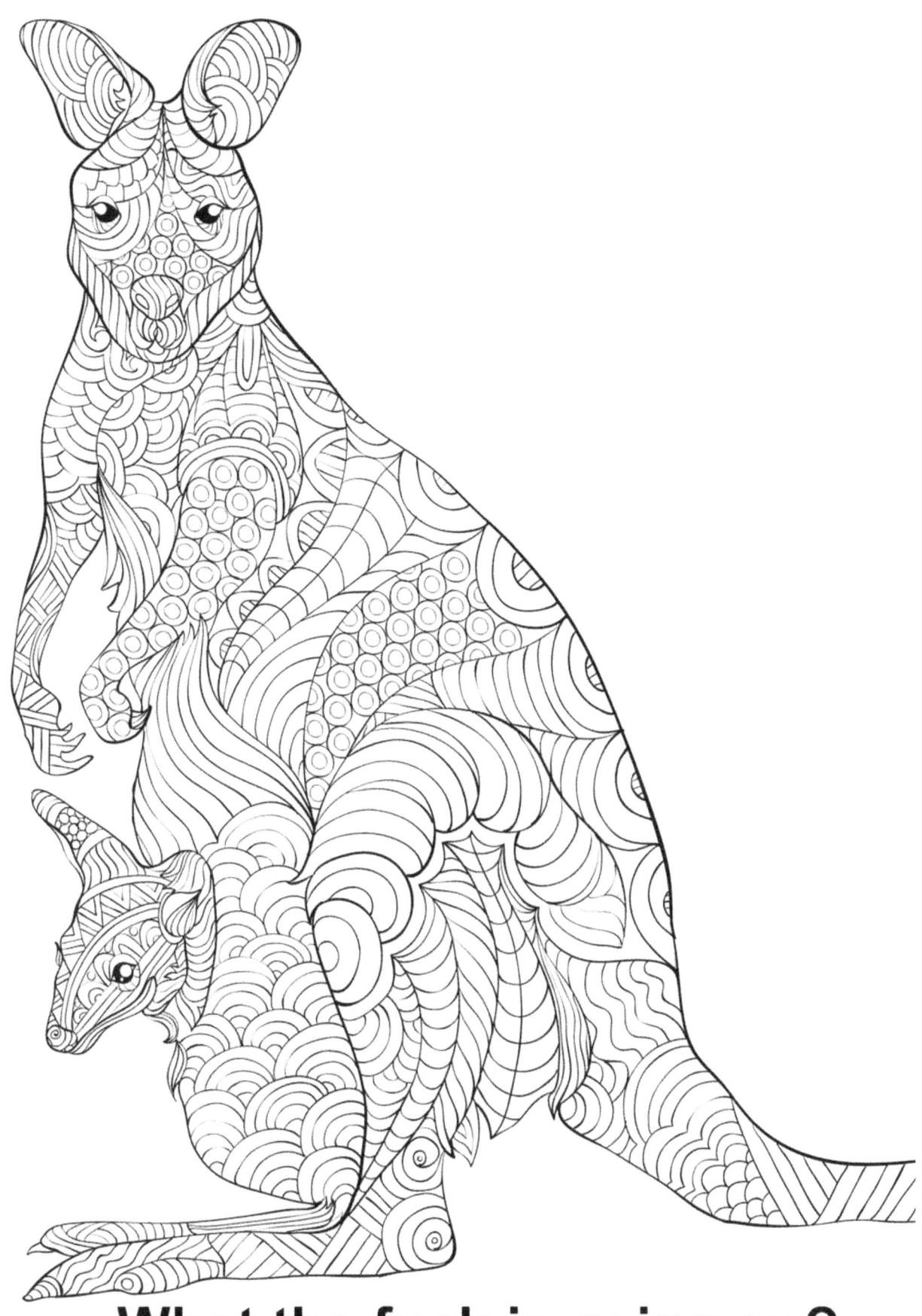

**What the fuck is going on?
You're not swearing!**

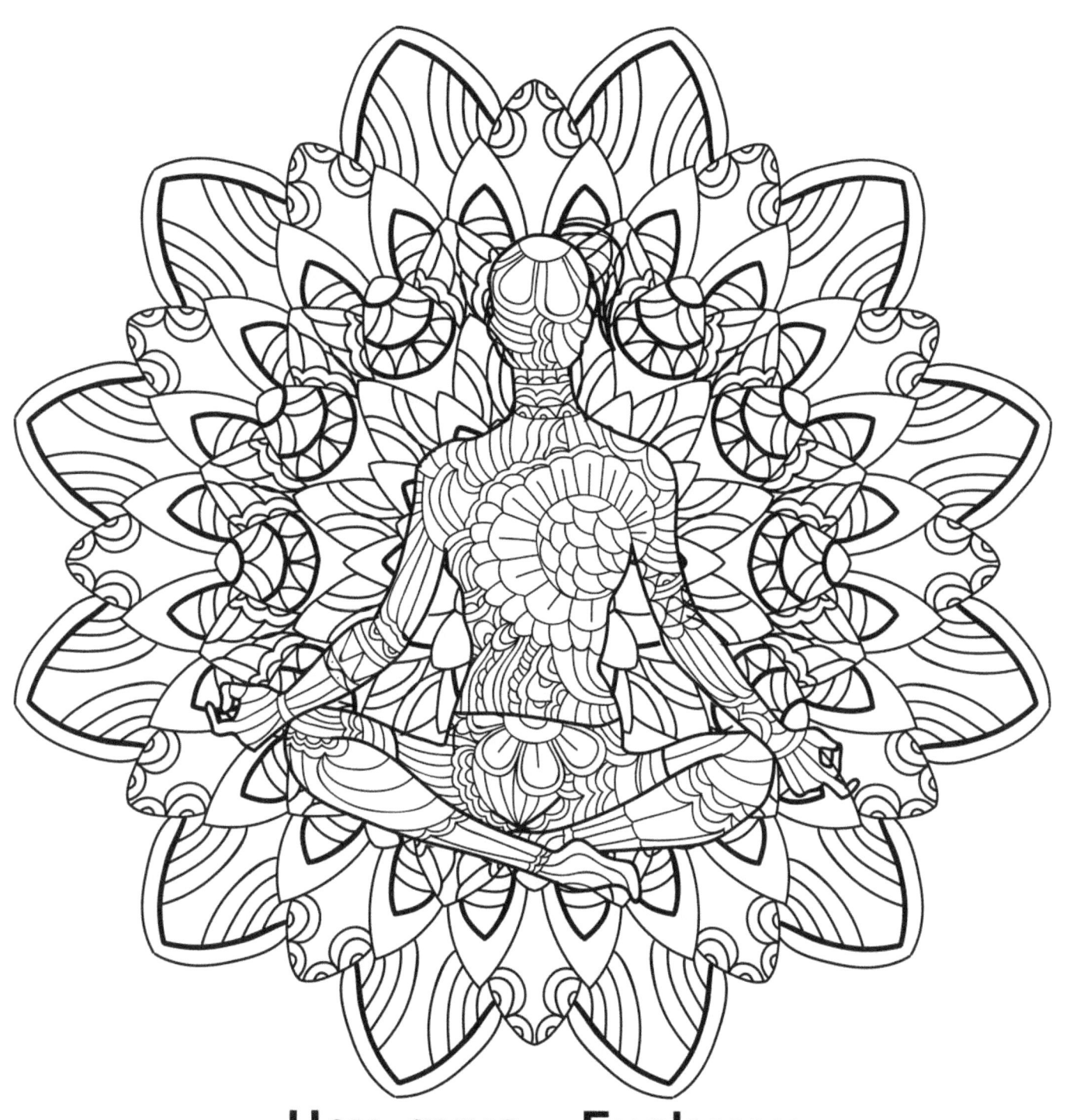

Hey, guys... Fuck you.

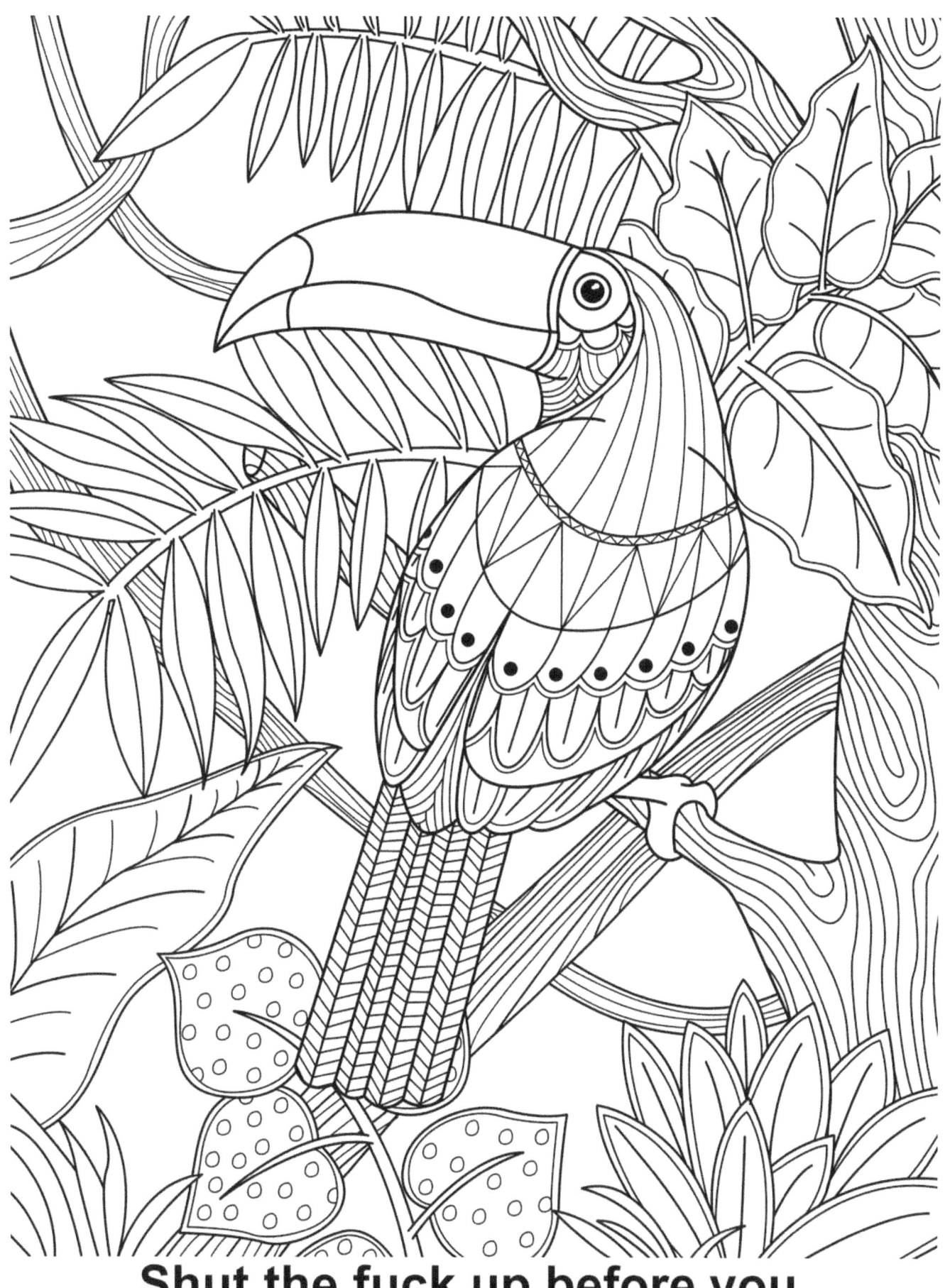

Shut the fuck up before you can swear.

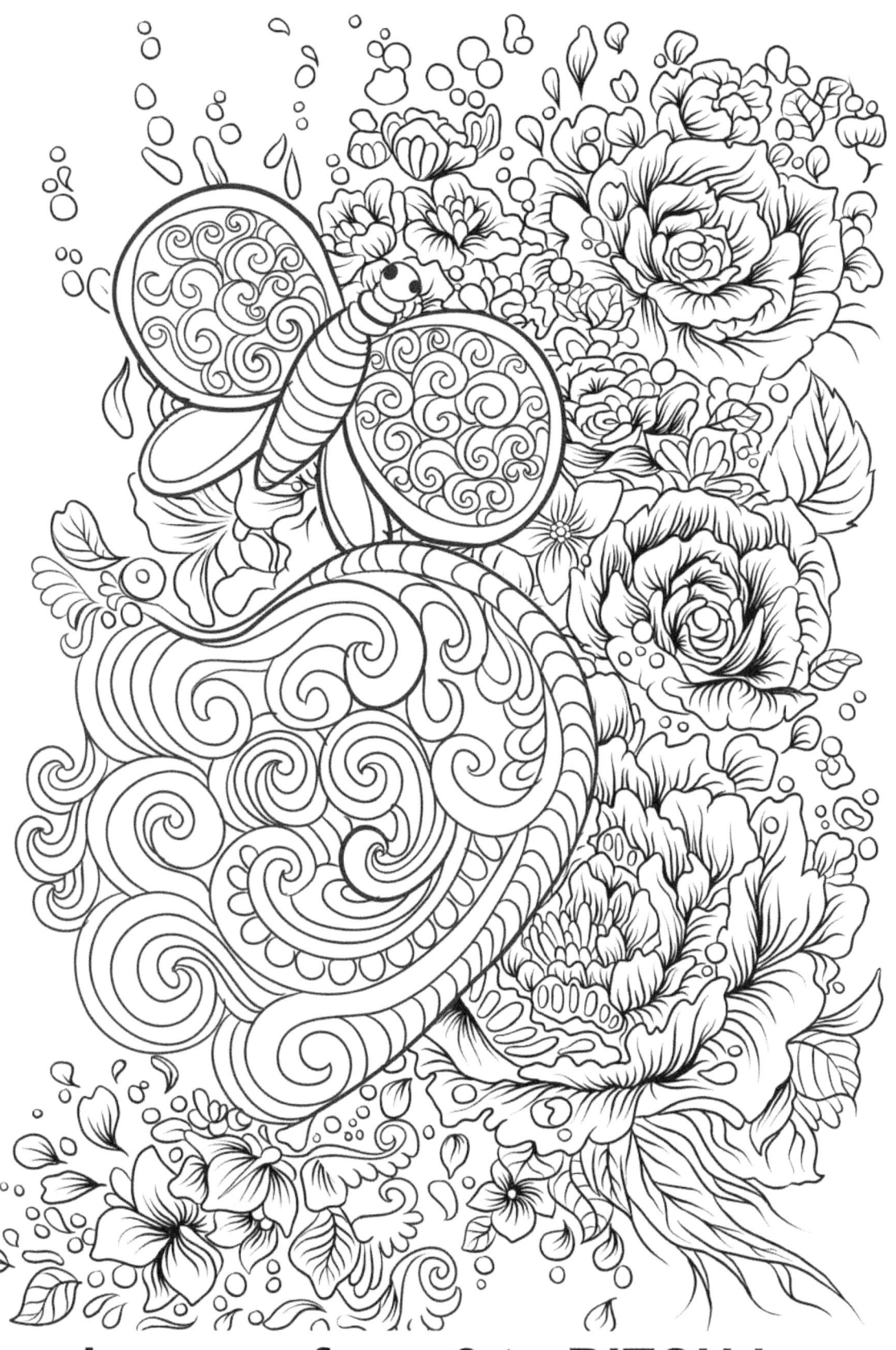

I can go from 0 to BITCH in
0.2 seconds. Go fucking
figure out.

www.ingramcontent.com/pod-product-compliance
Lightning Source LLC
Chambersburg PA
CBHW080641190526
45169CB00009B/3452